To my mom, the best in the world at building people up. I think she knows everyone has weaknesses, but she doesn't dwell on them.

Best Quotes and Affirmations for Kids
By Lindsey Michaels

Copyright © 2024 by Lindsey Michaels
ISBN 9798988186427

All rights reserved. No portion of this book may be used or reproduced in any matter whatsoever without written permission from the publisher. For permissions contact: Lmichaelsbooks@gmail.com

BEST QUOTES and Affirmations for Kids

The best and most beautiful things in the world cannot be seen or even touched, but just felt in the heart.

Helen Keller

My heart feels what is most important!

The harder the conflict, the more glorious the triumph.

Thomas Paine

I can work hard to accomplish something.

Curiosity is natural to the soul of man.

Daniel Boone

There are things I want to learn about because I am curious.

A life is not important except in the impact it has on other lives.

Jackie Robinson

I can make a difference in someone else's life.

I am not bound to win,
but I am bound to be true.
I am not bound to succeed,
but I am bound to live by
the light that I have.

Abraham Lincoln

Even if I don't win, I can still be proud of myself for doing my best.

Think of all the beauty still left around you and be happy.

Anne Frank

When I don't feel happy, I can still remember the good around me.

I leave this rule for others
when I'm dead:
Be always sure you're right,
and then go ahead.

David Crockett

I can take my time to make a plan that works. If my first plan doesn't work, I'll take my time to think through a new plan!

I always just thought
if you see somebody
without a smile,
give 'em yours!

Dolly Parton

I can make other people happy!

You have enemies? Good. That means you've stood up for something, sometime in your life.

Winston Churchill

I can do the right thing even if other people are choosing to do something else.

My hand trembles, but my heart does not!

Stephen Hopkins

Even when my body doesn't work perfectly, I'm still me!

Love yourself first and everything else falls into line.

Lucille Ball

I have my own special gifts and talents and can add so much goodness to the world!

Helen Keller became deaf and blind because of a serious illness when she was only 19 months old. Life was so hard for her, but a teacher named Anne Sullivan taught her to understand and use sign language. Helen learned Braille, went to college, became an author, and even learned to speak! You can find videos of her talking and you will see just how inspiring she is!

Thomas Paine was a writer whose words inspired people during the American Revolution even though it seemed impossible that they could win the war.

Daniel Boone explored the land west of the 13 American colonies and helped find the best path for others to follow.

Jackie Robinson was a gifted athlete in many sports as a kid, in college, and then as a professional. Once he started playing in Major League Baseball, he won the Rookie of the Year Award, the MVP Award, was a six time All-Star, and won the World Series with the Brooklyn Dodgers. With all of this success, he is best known for being the first black player in MLB. He had a lot of support but also a lot of opposition as he paved the way for change.

Abraham Lincoln failed many times and lost several elections, but changed the world for good as president of the United States. During his presidency, slavery in the USA ended and the country stayed united after the American Civil War.

Anne Frank was a girl whose family hid from the Nazis for two years during World War II. During that time, she wrote in a journal that she got for her thirteenth birthday. Her writing is so inspiring that it has been translated into over 70 languages and the annex where she hid was turned into a museum.

David Crockett lived such an adventurous life on the American frontier that many stories were written about him and he became very famous. Some stories about him are exaggerated but he did live a bold, daring life. (He is better known today as Davy Crockett, but he went by David.)

Dolly Parton has accomplished too much to fit on this page, but one special thing to know is that she started *Dolly Parton's Imagination Library*. Her dad never learned to read or write, and that inspired her idea to send free books to ALL of the kids living where she grew up. She started in Tennessee, and Dolly's *Imagination Library* is now sending free books to kids all around the world!

Winston Churchill was the prime minister of England during World War II. He played an important role, joining with other countries to defeat the Axis powers and preserve freedom.

Stephen Hopkins was a signer of the Declaration of Independence. He was one of the oldest men there, and his hand trembled so much that he normally had someone write things down for him. When John Adams offered to sign Stephen Hopkins' name for him, he said, "No! I will sign it myself—if we are hung for signing it, you shall not be hung for it for me." Then he used his left hand to steady his wrist, signed his name, and said the quote you find in this book. John Adams said this "electrified all Congress, and made the most timid firm in their purpose."

Lucille Ball is known for her success on *I Love Lucy*, an American television show that people loved right away. She was hilarious! Growing up, a lot of people told her that her ideas wouldn't work, but she didn't let negative opinions stop her from reaching her dreams.

www.ingramcontent.com/pod-product-compliance
Lightning Source LLC
Chambersburg PA
CBHW040724060526
44119CB00083B/313